HOW TO MAKE IT TO THE NBA

THE 100% TRUTH ABOUT COMING FROM NOWHERE, HAVING LITTLE TO NO SCHOLARSHIP OFFERS, AND STILL MAKING IT TO THE BIGGEST STAGE IN BASKETBALL

TO: D J

Always believe in Yourself!!

DONTELL JEFFERSON

Disclaimer

All the material contained in this book is provided for educational and informational purposes only. No responsibility can be taken for any results or outcomes resulting from the use of this material. While every attempt has been made to provide information that is both accurate and effective, the author does not assume any responsibility for the accuracy or use/misuse of this information.

Acknowledgements

Altanese Williams—Thank you for having the will and desire to want better for yourself and your son at a very young age. You have given me the support and foundation to go follow my dreams. I love you!

Jasmine S. McGowan — To my wonderful editor, thank you for turning my journey into a masterpiece.

Suresh May—Hearing about your life's challenges and how you turned it all around gave me the inspiration to tell my story. I am truly grateful for your advice and support for this project.

Marvin Collier, Laura Clark, Charlie Clark,

Kerry Sandifer, Robert Pritchett, Ronnie Thompson, Derrick Powell, Dave Joerger, Brad Jones, Larry Brown. You all have been an integral part of my success. Thank you for believing in me.

All of my former teams, coaches, teammates, and even players I thought were better than me, thank you. Without you NONE of this would be possible.

Last but not least, I beg forgiveness of all those who have been with me over the course of the years and whose names I failed to mention. Charge it to my head and not my heart. I love you all!

Testimonial

There are many people who could talk about how great a person Dontell Jefferson is, and he truly is a great person, but not many were fortunate to see his work ethic in his younger days. I vividly remember a time when Dontell used to come back and train, and he'd often call and ask me to come rebound for him or help him run drills, and I obliged because he was one of my best friends. I remember one time we were in the gym and his phone rang. I said, "Dontell, your phone is ringing." Dontell replied, "I'm at work." He didn't even think about answering his phone because basketball was most important to him at that time. He was working! This anecdote illustrates the dedication and discipline he had to keep getting better and honing his craft. He wouldn't even let a small distraction such as a ringing phone deter him, he just kept working. This Is something anyone interested in playing professionally needs to understand: it's hard work! I'll always value and admire Dontell's hard work and dedication. I'm proud of his journey and grateful to call him my friend.

Suresh May, best-selling author and founder of Wealth Weekly.

Table of Contents

VI

Introduction

Do you want to attend a MAJOR university to play D1 Ball? Are you clueless about how athletic scholarships and recruitment processes work? Do you have lofty dreams of playing in the NBA, seeing your name splashed across magazines, and having your face plastered on billboards? Or maybe you're just interested in an NBA player's story of how he made it, overcoming all the obstacles life set for him. This book will give you answers to all of these questions and more. You'll learn the truth about how to go pro and read of the dedication and drive needed to follow your dreams. Most importantly, you'll learn that no matter your situation, your goals can be achieved! This book will teach you how to handle the recruitment process from high school to college/university, as well as how to pick the right agent when you decide to turn pro. I'll even talk about a few life lessons I learned along the way in an effort to help you avoid some mistakes I've made. I wrote this book because I want to help a kid who has the same dreams I had growing up. In each chapter, you'll learn about my career, things I did to handle difficult situations, and how you can avoid those situations altogether. Are you ready for the TRUTH? Let's get started!

SECTION 1:

How to Come from Nowhere and Start Your Basketball Dream

Your "roots," or your life's foundation, can go very far in shaping how you'll eventually turn out. Cordele, Georgia, known as "The Watermelon Capital of the World," is a small town that lies in the shade of Atlanta; it's also where I was born. There aren't many tourist attractions or reasons to visit Cordele, but it's where I called home, and it's where it all started for me. One thing many would say about living in a small town is that it can limit you a bit. Some believe that small towns often produce small-minded people,

1

and this can be true in many cases. Sometimes living in a tiny bubble restricts the size of your dreams and limits you from thinking big. You also aren't typically exposed to different ideas and lifestyles when you live in a small town, be them good or bad. And while living in a small town can give you the "big fish in a little pond" type of fame, small towns can't always offer you the opportunity and exposure of bigger cities. I would never look down on anyone from a small town, nor do I feel that you should forget where you come from, but the exposure offered by a big city is unparalleled.

When you live in a bigger, more diverse city,

the different experiences you have and people you meet broaden your horizons. You start to believe that anything you can imagine is possible. Those small town limitations begin to fade away and you envision what your life can really be. For a sport like basketball, I think a big city is needed if you want to attract any real attention. I'm not saying you should look at your small town with spite for not being able to generate the traction you need to display your talents on a bigger stage; I'm simply saying you should go where you need to go to ensure your talent is noticed.

Cordele, Georgia is in the United States of America, the great land of opportunities!

But in Cordele, opportunities are not aplenty and career paths are limited. Once you successfully make it out of Cordele, you become a role model. Lots of people will look up to you. But I'm getting a little ahead of myself here. Let's rewind.

My mother, Altanese, had me when she was only fifteen. And because my mother was still a child herself when I was born, I lived with my grandmother and grandfather until my mom turned 21 and got her first apartment. My mom was working and going to college when she decided that living outside of Cordele would give both of us more opportunities. So I lived with my grandmother for another year while my mom left to set up a life for us in Atlanta. My grandmother, Laura, was a very religious and disciplined woman. A lot of my mom's childhood friends would even call her downright mean! My grandmother was strict, but she ran her household with love. If she said do something, you'd better hop up and get it done! You didn't operate on your own time, you'd better move when she said move! We spent every Sunday in Sunday school and church services. I may have hated some of my grandmother's rules back then, but she laid the foundation for discipline and structure that I'd need later in life.

My mom had one brother and I had several

aunts and uncles on my father's side. I spent most days after school hanging with my uncles, and they instilled a resilient and fighting spirit in me. In addition to my uncles, I also hung out and played football with a bunch of male cousins. We'd play football all day long in the middle of the street in front of my dad's mother's house; this is how I developed my competitive spirit. We'd play and compete against each other, not fully understanding the invaluable life lessons we were learning, and not fully aware that we were preparing ourselves for a life in competitive sports.

Though my mother was never really into sports, she always supported my dreams and nurtured my talents. She also did as much as she could to align me with people who could help me realize my dreams. Most of what I learned early on about truly developing as an athlete came from my one of my uncles, Willie (Frank) Collier. He'd attended the University of Pittsburgh as a wide-receiver, where he won a National Championship. He also played in the AFL (American Football League) for the Pittsburgh Stars, in the Canadian Football League where he won a Grey Cup, and had stints with the Pittsburgh Steelers and New Orleans Saints. Most of my determination, never- say-die spirit, and competitive nature came from him. Having my mother's support and my uncle's guidance were pivotal to my success as a basketball player.

In Cordele, Georgia, "The Watermelon Capital of the World," my father, Marvin, was well-known for playing football. So I naturally took to football as well and had no thoughts of basketball at the time. I used to watch Joe Montana and wanted to be an NFL quarterback. I played football from ages five through fourteen. I decided to stop playing in eighth grade after the football season ended. Looking back, I think I stopped playing football because I didn't want to be like my father. I had so much resentment due to his lack of communication and not being around while I was growing up that I wanted to play an entirely different sport from him. Shortly after eighth grade ended, I began to think about playing basketball in college. My father had set high school records in Cordele, then he went on to set even more records in college at Middle Tennessee State. Basketball allowed me to step out of my father's shadow, blaze my own trail, and set my own records. Transitioning over to basketball from football proved to be one of the best decisions I've ever made. I became determined to make a name for myself, and to set my own records without the added pressure of living up to my father's career. But, once again, I'm getting ahead of myself!

"Life in the Big City"

The summer of 1994, right before I began the fourth grade, I joined my mother in Atlanta. With a new school, new neighborhood, and no other family nearby, I was often homesick. I remember wanting to move back to Cordele so badly, but my grandmother wouldn't let me. At the time, my grandmother told me that I needed to be with my mom so I could protect her in the big city, but I knew she really just wanted to show my mom that she could handle raising me full-time. Shortly after moving to Atlanta and not finding any football rec leagues, I was introduced to organized basketball. I often played basketball in the yard back in Cordele or at another friend's house but it was never an organized game. Here is where the big city comes into play: in Atlanta I was able to meet diverse groups of teammates and coaches, which helped to make me a well-rounded person, both on and off the court. My mother put me in all sorts of recreational basketball leagues, the most notable being at Smyrna Community Center. I placed first in the skills test three years in a row and even won a championship my very first year of playing! I played both football and basketball in seventh and eighth grade until I decided to exclusively play basketball. I was going to high school, and my confidence and skills as a basketball player were truly developing. Even though my mom expected me to play football because she felt I was a better quarterback than basketball player, I felt in my heart that basketball was what I should be focused on in high school so I could play in college. I wanted to be a basketball star!

"Full-Time Hoop Dreams"

Adjusting to basketball wasn't very difficult for me. I'd always been athletic, and I knew a lot about the game from my rec teams. I'd simply never had any real coaching until I got to high school. Though I was determined to be one of the best on my team, I was frail, skinny, and a lot weaker than my teammates. But after having a growth spurt, at least I had a little height! I grew up in an environment with rough-and-tumble cousins and uncles, and I was used to being one of the little guys.

I wasn't afraid to go up against bigger or even more skilled players, because I knew that playing with those guys would only make me better. More importantly, I knew that eventually *I'd* be one of the best. I never let fear deter me.

I was never the type of kid to back down. If I lost, I'd come back the next day, the next hour, hell I'd even ask for a rematch right after losing! What I lacked in physical strength, I made up for in mental fortitude. I always had the drive and the willpower necessary to succeed at basketball, I just needed the skills and physical strength to match.

When my peers were worried about zits and pubescent hormones, I was more concerned with proving myself on the court. I was so nervous to try out for the Stephenson High School junior varsity team because my skills were a lot poorer than the other guys. I thought I played horribly during tryouts! Thankfully, albeit surprisingly, I made the team! Making the team was one of my proudest moments at the time, and I was so excited to begin my *real* basketball career! However, when the season rolled around, I was rarely allowed to play. I worked my butt off to improve, but I still couldn't get ahead of my teammates. I rode the bench, game after game. Incidentally, years later, I learned that my junior varsity coach didn't even want me on the team. I was only picked because the varsity coach, Coach Kerry Sandifer, saw something in me. I'm not sure what Coach Sandifer saw in me at the time, but I'm eternally grateful for his foresight. Anyway, even though I rarely played that year, my team won the Dekalb County Championship! When the junior varsity season ended, Coach Sandifer moved me to the varsity team to finish out their season. As a freshman, this gave me an unprecedented boost of experience and confidence. I got to play with much bigger, much older, more experienced varsity players, and my game improved dramatically. I played out of position as a power forward my sophomore year and little of my junior year. I was a 6'1" kid weighing 155lbs playing as a power forward in my sophomore year! Most power forwards are typically stronger and taller than 6'1", so I was in a little over my head, to say the least. I personally didn't think I'd be productive in this position because I was naturally a guard, but me playing power forward created match-up problems for opposing teams. Playing power forward also helped me at times because I'd often be matched with a slower defender. I'd bring the defender out to the wing (outside the three-point line) and play to my strength of driving the ball to the basket. There was also sometimes a disadvantage to me playing power forward because I wasn't a good post defender, so I often defended guards. But no matter my position, I was intent on getting better. My goal of being one of the best was still heavy on my mind!

My team became a lot better during my junior year of high school. This was a great thing for us, and not only because we began to win more games and experienced a confidence boost. When our team improved, better, more competitive teams were willing to play us. We all know you can't become the best until you play with the best, so playing with more experienced teams was a great catalyst for our team's growth. Our team's improvement also allowed my coach to play me at the shooting guard/small forward position, where I thrived. I'd always felt I should have been the shooting guard/small forward, so I was happy to finally be in that position. Coach Sandifer may not initially have had the very best players on his team, but he worked hard to bring out the best in all of us. We played well together, we did our best, and we had fun doing it. My teammates were like my brothers. We played hard and gave 110% every game.

During my senior year, just when we'd really found our groove, my team encountered a setback. Our starting point guard dislocated his shoulder, forcing us to switch up a few positions and line ups. As I was the next best ball handler on the team, my coach moved me to point guard. Little did I know at the time that this position change would eventually lead me to the NBA! Funny thing is, I was always told that I'd never be a point guard, so I never worked as hard as I probably should have on my ball handling back then. Because of this, becoming my team's point guard wasn't exactly a smooth transition for me. The workload for my team was very heavy as I had to quickly learn how to score, get everyone in position for the plays, and know what was happening on the floor at all times. However, as I'd always been an unselfish player, setting up guys and passing was the easy part. And as always, I was determined to be the best. Although I really hated that our point guard dislocated his shoulder, I'm also proud of how we overcame that obstacle as a team. One thing I know for sure is if I would have known then what I know now, I would have spent way more time working on my ball handling skills and going harder in the gym! Though my current knowledge can't help my teenaged self, I hope my life lessons can help you up-and-coming athletes out there!

"The AAU Experience"

In addition to playing basketball for my high

school, I also played AAU, or Amateur Athletic Union, basketball. I started with my first AAU team, the Georgia Rockets, my freshman year of high school. I initially only joined an AAU team because a few of my friends from high school had joined the Rockets. My first year of playing AAU, I was only interested in having fun and spending extra time playing basketball with my friends. I didn't really take AAU seriously; I was just happy being around my friends and playing basketball outside of school.

The summer going into my junior year, a few of my friends and I got picked to play with The Worldwide Entertainment Renegades (now Game Elite), a very dominant AAU team. Playing for Worldwide allowed us to travel to a lot of different cities and play against some of the nation's most prominent young players at the time, such as Bracey Wright and Corey Brewer, many who went on to be drafted into the NBA. Although Worldwide was a dominant basketball program, we didn't have star names or huge college/NBA prospects, so playing against relatively famous high school athletes pushed us to go toe-to-toe with players who were deemed better than us. We fought every game to shut down the hype of those big names! Even when we didn't win, we were always comfortable knowing we'd made an impression. We refused to let the big names intimidate us, and we made sure that they remembered *our* names by the end of the game!

Earlier that same summer, a few of my high school teammates and I decided to have our own AAU team. We all spoke with Coach Sandifer, and he also thought it was a good idea, so he asked our assistant coach, Coach Rod, to be our AAU coach. Coach Rod agreed, and during the AAU season, we'd run the same plays from the high school season. Running those familiar plays allowed me to see some of the guys play differently than what I was used to in high school. It seems that some of those guys just needed a challenge! For this reason, I champion AAU basketball. It forces you out of your comfort zone and demands your best. If you can play, then you can truly play against anybody. AAU puts your skills to the test! So though I initially didn't care about AAU ball at all, and I know some people are totally against it, I understand that AAU can be both a gift and a curse. A lot of times kids join AAU teams for the free shoes and travel, but they'll hardly ever play. Some people play in the very demanding league and end up with nothing to show for it because no one gets to see their talents. Despite its shortcomings, AAU basketball helped me to sharpen my skills and develop even more lifelong friendships. I developed a camaraderie with new guys, and strengthened friendships with my high school teammates. We were all very close, and we hung out a lot.

"Story time"

Though I demand respect and play with confidence on the court, I'd always been a bit shy off the court. My teammates helped me to become a bit more outspoken and less reserved. I vividly remember driving my mother's car with four of my teammates, listening to music, trying to freestyle rap on our way to an AAU tournament game!

I can't say that I would have done anything like that before my basketball friendships. We were just a bunch of 16 and 17 year-old kids just enjoying life. We focused on playing good basketball, having fun, and nothing else. We were together all the time, as teammates and as brothers. We weren't so concerned about winning or losing, because we knew that no matter what, we played hard and gave our very best at every game. Playing AAU basketball with my high school teammates just made it that much more fun and memorable. It was so much fun competing against guys like Dwight Howard and Josh Smith, who were high school freshmen or sophomores on the Atlanta Celtics AAU team, with my high school teammates.

We knew we were witnessing greatness in

the making, and we gave greatness right back. Competing with my high school teammates as an AAU team brought a long-lasting, indelible joy. Even with all the places I've been, experiences I've had, and people I've met, playing AAU basketball with my best friends invokes some of my fondest memories.

There are so many stories I could tell and memorable games I could talk about from my years at Stephenson High School. There's nothing like the pure, untainted adrenaline and enjoyment of high school sports. I could go on and on, but I'll just discuss a few more of my unforgettable moments:

Around February of my senior year, we

played a game versus Berkmar, then the #1 school in the state. They had Wayne Arnold, who was Mr. Georgia Basketball 2002, on their roster. We were the home team, so we had the crowd and momentum in our favor. We were down by two points with five minutes left in the game. Imagine our hysteria! We had those guys on the ropes! In the last few minutes of the game, fueled by a mad desire to win, Coach Sandifer received a technical foul. Though that foul deflated us a bit and we ended up losing the game by six points, it was a turning point for our team. This game was a testament to our coach's ability to make the best out of setbacks, as this was after our point guard dislocated his shoulder. Coming so close to a victory against the #1 team in the state restored our confidence and made all other teams know that we were a force to be reckoned with!

Another time, on Senior Night, we were down by nine points against Tri- Cities High School with only about two minutes left in the game. It was the last home game of the season. Everyone in the crowd might have thought all hope was lost, but I refused to lose our last game! Unlike the Berkmar game, where we feverishly and unsuccessfully tried to win, a calm and a poise came over me. I made three 3-point shots in a row and sent the game into overtime! We kept our focus and managed to shut down the other team, ending with a victory! Looking back, I think that game really showed the kind of player I could be; it showed the kind of player I *wanted* to be. It was when I truly began to understand the depth of character, heart, and performance under pressure needed to be a player worth admiring.

As I've said, I was once following in my father's footsteps. I wanted to play football and become a quarterback in the NFL. I definitely did not see myself being where I am today. Those football dreams all changed, of course, when I fell in love with basketball.

"Seeing the Goal"

My former stepfather, Ronald, who married my mom when I was 14 years old, spent a few years playing in the NFL for the Cincinnati Bengals. He gave me all sorts of useful advice that I still adhere to today. He once said, "If you have a goal, write it down and post it somewhere you'll see it every day. Then do all you can to work towards it!" I took his advice to heart, and I still post my goals to this very day. My goals were to go to the University of North Carolina to play basketball, to lead my conference in scoring, and to make it to the NBA. I wrote those goals down in big, bold letters with a black Sharpie, then posted them on the back of my closet door. I'd reread my goals every day while getting dressed, then I'd march out, reminding myself to continue to work towards them. As we know, I didn't accomplish all of my initial goals. But I *did* accomplish perhaps the loftiest goal of all: I became an NBA player!

One thing I want everyone to get from reading this: don't be afraid to set big goals! Virtually nothing is impossible with hard work. Absorb and implement all the good advice, and ignore all naysaying comments. Once you know what you really, truly want to do, take every step you can to better yourself and put yourself in a position to be successful. Most importantly, surround yourself with people who support your dreams. Get rid of negativity, and align yourself with people who truly believe in you. As you get more serious about what you want to do in life, you have to not only align yourself with people who are supportive of your dreams, you also have to *position yourself* around people who *share* your dreams, or who can *help you* achieve those dreams. In high school, you don't really think about getting to the next level. You're in the moment, having fun with your teammates. As you really begin to think about a career in sports, you have to understand the seriousness behind not only performing well on the court, but off the court as well. Seek out people who have solid plans of playing professionally, treat your body as a machine by working out, eating healthy, and abstaining from drugs and alcohol, and stay away from all illegal activity, or anything that will tarnish your image and reputation. The sooner you *take* your sport seriously after high school, the sooner you'll be *taken* seriously in your sport after high school. So what's next for a high school graduate who's serious about his sport? Well, if you're anything like me, with little to no scholarship offers, there might be a few bumps ahead! No worries, though. I'm going to tell you how to drive right over those bumps to get where you want to go!

SECTION 2:

How to Go to a Big-Time NCAA D1 Program with Little to No Scholarship Offers

Most of us are shielded from a lot of real world situations from birth until high school. Your parents typically take care of everything, and your only job is to be a good student and to try your best at anything you attempt. Reality hits many of us very hard after we graduate, and we have to make some serious, grown-up decisions about how we want the rest of our lives to go. Some of us choose college, some of us choose the military, and some of us go directly into the workforce. i f you're someone who wants to play professional basketball, you have a few options. If you're a top high school prospect like Lebron James or Dwight Howard, then you're set! Enter the draft and enjoy your career in the NBA! However, if you're like the vast majority of high school players who want to one day play professionally, the next move is going to college on an athletic scholarship. But what happens when you don't have any scholarship offers? Do you give up on basketball and abandon the goals you've set for yourself? Absolutely not.

"Life in Junior College"

The journey after high school graduation was a little difficult for me. I'd taken the SAT three times and the ACT once and just got tired of taking the tests, and though my GPA was acceptable for the NCAA Clearinghouse, my test scores always came up a little short. I'd received one division offer from Morris Brown College in Atlanta, and one other offer from a junior college, which I knew nothing about. I knew I didn't want to go to Morris Brown because I'd have to sit out a year because I didn't meet the Clearinghouse requirements, so I decided to look into junior college where I received a scholarship offer from a local school in Atlanta. My mother had gotten married in the summer of 1998. My stepfather had a friend whom he'd played football with at Clemson University who'd gone to junior college. My stepfather's friend was able to tell me the ins and outs of being a junior college athlete and what it could mean for the rest of my basketball journey. After weighing my options, I chose to attend Atlanta Metropolitan College (now Atlanta Metropolitan State College). This ended up being one of the smartest and most important decisions I've made concerning basketball.

Attending Atlanta Metro was a great decision because it allowed me the opportunity to work on my shortcomings as a player and prepare for higher-leveled college basketball. I got to play with older, stronger, more experienced players, and this helped my game immensely. Junior college also allowed me to adjust to a typical college class workload while being an athlete.

Regarding my living conditions, living in a dorm wasn't the easiest of transitions. I was used to having my own room and a big bed at home. I wasn't used to sharing personal space and always having someone in my room. We had full beds my freshman year at Atlanta Metro, but we had twin beds during my sophomore year, and I had to share my space with even more people! I had a roommate and suitemates, which was basically like having four people share a two-bedroom apartment. And we only had one bathroom! It was tough at first, but I will say it brought us closer as friends and teammates. We were around each other all the time; in the dorms, during study hall, and of course at practice. The situation wasn't always ideal, but it definitely helped to foster a brotherhood amongst all the players.

My game immediately got into a groove at Atlanta Metro, largely due to my coach, Robert Pritchett, and his structured practicing style. We did the exact same thing every day in practice. Coach believed that doing the same thing every day was the only way for us to get better. Every day we'd stretch and run a drill Coach called "alley ball," also known as "zigzag one-on-one." After alley ball, we'd do an outlet drill. Outlet drills involve two players, and a third to throw the ball (this was Coach in our case). Coach would throw the ball off the backboard, one player would rebound and pass it to the other player, then both players would sprint down the floor where the rebounder would receive a pass for a lay up. Outlet drills were followed by shooting drills. We'd go from the baseline to the free throw line and shoot jumpers, over and over again. Finally, after all of those initial drills, we'd scrimmage. Each team would play ten minutes on defense, ten minutes on offense, and twenty minutes full court. The great thing about these in-practice games is that the coaches didn't call anything. I say it was a great thing, but those practices were grueling! There were no out of bounds or foul calls during these games, which means everything was fair play. Running the games this way helped to create a more aggressive and competitive atmosphere. We never complained about fouls because there *were* no fouls. We were prepared to face anything in a real game, and would never whine about things not being called.

When I began at Atlanta Metro, my biggest deficiency as a player was that I wasn't a consistent shooter. I could always score, was long enough, and I had an ardent desire to play defense, but I was majorly lacking in becoming a consistent jump shooter. Doing those daily shooting drills, along with practicing my shots in my free time, greatly improved my consistency as a shooter.

I honestly didn't have to make many changes academically when I went to Atlanta Metro. Junior college was basically like high school all over again: I went to class, had study hall from 3:30pm to 5:00pm, then had an hour break until practice at 6:00pm. I'd get most of my work done during study hall, so I was typically free after practice. It wasn't a bad schedule at all.

I did have one setback in junior college, and it was because of a mistake of my own doing: I never declared a major! I knew I wanted to work with computers, but I didn't know exactly what I wanted to do. So, I never declared a major. I had to spend two years at Atlanta Metro because I was a Prop 48, which meant I didn't have the necessary test scores to leave after my freshman year. So not declaring a major came back to bite me once I declared for University of Arkansas. I had to declare a major and make sure I graduated on time to be eligible in the fall. So my advice to you guys: continue to take the SAT/ACT until you meet the NCAA Clearinghouse requirements, and if you begin in junior college, declare a major as soon as possible!

I had a great career at Atlanta Metropolitan, and actually got a lot of exposure. When I was a freshman, one of my sophomore teammates, Richard Jeter, was being highly recruited and watched by NBA scouts. He eventually declared for the NBA draft. This was great for me, as it allowed me to get seen early on by NBA scouts and major universities. I averaged around 17 points, 6 assists, 4 rebounds, and 3 steals per game during my freshman year, and 16.4 points, 9.2 assists, 6.7 rebounds, and 3.4 steals as a sophomore. I was a two-year starter and MVP of the team two years in a row. I definitely made my presence known, and was sure I could play on the next level. Atlanta Metro may have initially seemed like a bit of a detour leaving high school, but it ended up being just what I needed to reaffirm that professional basketball really was a possibility for me.

I can't really put my feelings about my time at Atlanta Metropolitan into words. It afforded me opportunities and opened doors I never thought possible of a junior college. At the time I really wished Atlanta Metro was a four-year school for athletics. It was such an amazing place to cultivate my skills. We had a great team and it was just so much fun! This was probably the last time I was virtually carefree as athlete.

"Division 1 Adjustments"

Going from junior college basketball at Atlanta Metro to D1 ball was quite an adjustment. I had a wealth of experience, and was very tall and athletic, but I still wasn't as physically strong as my teammates or fellow opponents. I was still very skinny back then and smaller and weaker than everyone else. I remember taking my official visit to the University of Arkansas and seeing Tony Allen of the opposing team, who was playing for Oklahoma State at the time. Dude was huge! After seeing how big he was, I took a good look at myself and knew I needed to get in the weight room. Bulking up and catching up to my peers' size and strength was a major adjustment I had to make when I went to D1 basketball.

I'd put myself in a very decent position coming out of junior college. For this reason, I had a lot more options leaving Atlanta Metro than when I'd left high school. Clemson, Colorado, Florida State, Arkansas, and Georgia were all places that were interested in me. Anywhere in Georgia was out because I wanted to finally get out of my home state. My first and only school visit was to the University of Arkansas. I'd known about some of the traditions just from watching them on TV as a kid, but being there was a totally different experience. Being in the arena and witnessing the Razorbacks' fans' passion made me feel like the University of Arkansas was the place I wanted to be. It seems like my decision was a lot easier to make than a few of my highly-recruited teammates. Arkansas just felt right. I declared in December of my sophomore year because I didn't want to go the full season not knowing or having the burden of going where I didn't really want to go.

Even though I knew Arkansas was the school for me after one visit, I'd advise you to take all your visits. Embrace recruiting because if you go through the process coming out of high school, you'll only have that experience once. One plus side of going to a junior college or prep school is that you'll (ideally) be recruited all over again for a four-year school, but again, definitely take all your visits, enjoy meeting new people, enjoy being recruited.

While enjoying the fun and excitement of the recruitment process, pay attention! Take note of your potential team's playing style, how your game would fit within their style, and if you could handle the distance from home.

You may cross a few schools off your list because they're too far away from *or* too close to home. Choose wisely. Deciding which college to attend will probably be your most important decision up to that point and will have a major impact on the rest of your life.

Once you've picked the perfect school for

you, prepare for a transition into early adulthood in a brand new environment.

The transition into college is a little different for everyone because of our different backgrounds. We come from different communities, have different values, and have lived different life experiences. Though we're all different, you can rest assured that each incoming freshman or transfer student is just as nervous to begin the journey as you are. My transition into Arkansas basketball was definitely not what I was expecting. Remember, not choosing my major left me a little behind. So the summer before I began at Arkansas, I had to go to summer school. I didn't even enroll at

Arkansas until after the summer as I had to meet the requirements first. This unfortunately meant that I missed out on Arkansas's summer weight program with strength and conditioning coach Kelly Lambert, which I desperately needed! But, despite those setbacks, I hit the ground running when the fall semester began. I put on 10lbs my first six weeks, hitting the weights as often as possible. I adapted to my demanding schedule as best I could. I had to juggle going to class everyday, weight-training, daily study halls, two practices a day with preseason workouts, and getting sufficient rest to do it all over again the next day!

Basketball came naturally for me at Arkansas, especially as I got stronger. SEC, or Southeastern Conference, basketball was a different level of basketball. It was a lot more intensive and demanded more than junior college ball, but I adapted quickly. I also had very supportive teammates who pushed me every day. I had to play behind Eric Ferguson for a while. He was very strong, quick, and a great competitor, so I'd definitely say he was someone who pushed me to perform at my best. Everyone on the Arkansas team and staff was encouraging and helpful. They wanted to see me do well and did all they could to help me be better. Through their kindness and encouragement,

I was constantly reminded that Arkansas was the team for me.

Adjusting to the classroom while at Arkansas was a cake walk. Coach Pritchett constantly stressed the importance of school, so I took full advantage of the study hall sessions and tools our coaches put in place to make my job in the classroom a lot easier. Combining basketball with classroom work can be difficult, especially if you already have a problem maintaining your grades *without* sports. If you want to get a head start, or if you ever feel your grades slipping, meet with a tutor. Never be ashamed of needing additional help, as that's what tutors are for. As a college athlete, your school has invested thousands of dollars for you to play. Don't jeopardize that by neglecting to use all of your resources.

No matter who you are, we are all given the same 24 hours per day. Where you end up in life largely depends on how well you manage your time. I'd definitely say time management was one of the most important keys to my success at Arkansas. I'd do my schoolwork during study hall, go to practice for about three hours, then go eat. After I'd eat with my teammates, we'd have free time. I just tried to make sure I got most of my important stuff done early before moving on to anything else. Remember, time management is key!

One additional time commitment that I didn't really have in junior college was community appearances. Most of these were held during the day and you'd know ahead of time, so they were easy to place in my schedule. These appearances were really cool because I got to meet a lot of the team's fans and feel the love and excitement of the community. Community appearances also taught me that I was playing basketball for more than myself and my family. Less fortunate people look up to us athletes. Some even idolize us. A lot of kids want to be us when they grow up, and a lot of adults look to us with pride. For these reasons, it's always important to be polite, smile, shake hands, take pictures, and encourage everyone you meet. You never know whose life you might change.

Of course, I wouldn't be keeping it all the way real without mentioning the college parties! Partying is a big thing at virtually every college, but especially those colleges with a huge athletic following. You're thrown in the middle of youthful exuberance with a lot of kids who are experiencing their first tastes of freedom! Once I got to Arkansas, I also experienced a taste of fame. I was always being invited to parties, always meeting new people. I definitely indulged from time to time, but partying was never really my thing. Many are probably surprised to hear that coming from an athlete, but it's true! It was always school, basketball, *then* partying for me. Again, you have to have your priorities and time management in order. Some people, especially athletes, will fail because their priorities are out of whack. Absolutely have fun and enjoy yourself, but make sure you keep your head on straight and your end goals in mind. I wouldn't trade those college days for anything!

College basketball is a business, but back then I was still just a carefree student athlete. It's a little different as a professional. When you're in college, you go to school, play ball, party, hang out with your friends, and do it all over again the next day. We didn't hang out as much or party as hard during the basketball season, because it was more demanding of our time, but we still didn't have a worry in the world. You just don't have much to think about. Professionally, it's a totally different ballgame because there's money involved in everything you do. So definitely live those college years to the fullest!

"Plans Change"

Every athlete has hopes and dreams entering college. We all have an idea of what we want to do, and where we want to end up. Some players just want to use their athletic talents for the college scholarship, and they never play basketball again after graduation. Some people want to play professionally overseas or in the NBA. Most guys have big dreams of becoming franchise players on popular teams. I had hopes and dreams about my career at Arkansas, but everything didn't turn out exactly as I wanted them to. I didn't start much as a junior and I started only the first half of my season as a senior. I wanted to win a national championship, but unfortunately, that never happened. I also wanted to average at least ten points with at least seven assists per game, but I left Arkansas averaging three points and five assists and a couple of steals. I didn't 100% accomplish everything I wanted to while at Arkansas, but

I'm still proud of my time there.

I think the highlights of my career were hitting some big free throws against Missouri, Ole Miss, and Tennessee that put us in the position to finish the season strong and make it to the NCAA tournament. I also set a single Arkansas game assist record with 15 assists my senior season, tying the previous record that had been established in the early 1990s by Kareem Reid. I'm proud of these things. I'm happy I was able to perform when I was called upon. I gained a lot of experience as a Razorback, and wouldn't take it back for the world.

Players often talk about having problems with their coaches. Having issues with your coach can really be a lot to deal with, but I think sometimes players are naive as to what's really happening. Guys talk about things the coach won't *let* them do, but sometimes you and the coach just have a different way of doing things, which can cause conflict. There are also instances where you do everything your coach asks of you and yet somehow still fall short of his vision. This was what happened in my case. After starting the first half of my senior season and playing well, I was told not to take certain shots and was pulled out of the game after every mistake, no matter how minor. I was eventually given little to no playing time every game. My confidence in myself and my skills plummeted.

I took being benched in stride. I didn't let it affect my interactions with my teammates, and I continued to perform to the best of my abilities. I went to practices on time and worked as hard as everyone else, and when I did get in the games, I played as hard as I could to help my team win. Being benched just spurred me to continue to do all I could to get where I wanted to be.

I remember having a meeting with my coach the summer after my senior season ended. I was in summer school finishing up my degree. He told me to finish school and play for the new ABA, or American Basketball Association, team that was coming to the city and not to worry about getting into the NBA. He'd told me if the NBA wanted me, they would have been calling him. Hearing that from my coach was really hard for me to process back then. But, it reinforced the fact that everyone will not support your dreams, everyone will not believe in your vision. Sometimes you just have to let people think whatever they want to think as you continue on your path to success. Again, it was hard being benched, especially when I knew I wasn't doing anything wrong. I was always going to practice and putting in extra work. It was also hard knowing my coach didn't believe I had what it took to make it to the NBA. Luckily, I continued to have the support and positivity of my teammates, especially my roommate, Ronnie Brewer. I knew I should've had more time off the bench, but it was out of my control. So for the rest of my time in college, I simply kept doing the things that got me to Arkansas in the first place, focused on my schoolwork, and had fun on and off the court with my teammates.

"The Phone Call"

When I finished school, I didn't have an agent. As luck would have it, one of my former assistant coaches, Ronnie Thompson, contacted me over the summer. During our initial conversation, I told him how I wanted to play professional basketball but didn't know any agents to help me. He just so happened to have an agent friend to connect me with. From there, the agent persuaded me to start off in the D-League, the NBA's minor or "development" league (now known as the NBA G League), because I eventually wanted to play in Europe. And that's how I ended up with an agent. I didn't even know how to get in contact with any agents, seeing as I wasn't a lottery pick or anything like that. Thanks to the relationship I had with Coach Thompson, a whole new world was opened up to me. This whole experience just served to remind me that building and maintaining relationships is always important. To think, if

I had been an asshole or lazy player, my old assistant coach wouldn't have thought to check in on me or help me get an agent. It's always important to build healthy professional relationships, especially when you're just hoping to start a career after college. You never know who might be able to help you a year, or even decades, down the line. I'll always be thankful to Ronnie Thompson because he helped usher me into the professional world of basketball.

How To Make It To The NBA

SECTION 3:

Dealing with Agents

A gents are the unsung heroes of professional sports. Athletes can't be everywhere at one time, nor can we represent ourselves in all capacities. As a basketball player, the need for an agent cannot be overemphasized. You need to have a trustworthy, savvy person always on the lookout for you, someone who always has your back. Agents are essential to your career's progression. With all that being said, dealing with agents has the potential to be a bit dicey. If your agent isn't properly looking out for you or if he or she is distracted by their other clients, your career might suffer. The right representation is essential to negotiating beneficial deals and trades. Your agent will basically determine whether you'll be getting a paycheck each month or not, so choose wisely.

Coming out of Arkansas in 2006, I didn't really know anyone familiar with agents or even the process of how to obtain one. Like I said, one of my assistant coaches connected me with his friend who eventually became my agent. My agent was able to help me understand my situation and options as a relatively unknown player who didn't have the stats some other guys had. From 2006 to January 2012, we worked together and had a good relationship. He helped me get drafted in the D-League, with hopes of working overseas in Europe, where I really wanted to begin my career. At the time, I didn't know anything about the D-League. I'd only first heard about it through my assistant coach and eventually my agent. The NBA's D-League helped pave the way for my career and gave me a start when I had very few options, so I'll always be thankful for that.

"Picking the Right Agent"

When picking an agent, even if you don't have many options, alway remember that your agent works for you, not the other way around. You should never feel like you work for your agent, or that your agent doesn't have your best interests at heart. If you do ever feel this way, you and your agent need to have a discussion about your concerns and talk about the direction he or she is trying to take your career.

If you don't have direct access to agents, contact friends, former teammates or other players, or coaches to see if they know anyone. Try to get your player reel from your school, make multiple copies for yourself and potential agents, and always have it at hand. Also, Google potential agents. A lot of agencies have a list of agents and their clients on their websites. In the very least, any potential agent of yours should have a social media presence. Really consider the number of clients an agent has. Going with an agent with a smaller number of clients might be the best bet for you because a lot of times players get lost and feel neglected when they sign with bigger agencies. This is especially true if you're not the player generating the most money for your agent. Do all you can to make an educated decision, consult with your support system, and go with your gut.

The process of getting an agent was very different for me. I was still in summer school finishing up my degree, and I had no idea how I was going to continue playing basketball. I had no prospects and no agents fighting for my business. I simply knew I wanted to keep playing ball and that I'd do whatever I could to make that happen. I didn't have any guidance or education about agents, and I really just took what I could get. I went with my first agent because I had no other options; he was the only one willing to give me an opportunity. For anyone who might be in a similar situation, don't lose hope. You have options! Finding an agent and getting yourself noticed is a lot easier now than it was when I was fresh out of college. Almost none of today's social media sites existed in 2006, but today you have Facebook, Twitter, LinkedIn, Instagram, and countless other tools at your fingertips to help you get noticed. Use these platforms to gain fans, connect with agencies, and garner the attention of people who can help to elevate your career.

"When the Unexpected Happens"

Once you've found an agent and a team, get ready to work your butt off! No matter how much work you put in, you will never be totally prepared for everything. An injury, for example, is something you'll never be prepared for. Injuries are particularly hard to deal with, because you'll want to be on the court with your team, doing way more than your injury dictates. I think the worst part about injuries is having surgery and going to rehab. Trying to recover from an injury is really hard for someone who's used to performing in top condition. Injuries not only affect you physically, they affect you mentally as well. You'll wonder if you'll be able to play as well as you could before the injury. Will your handles and agility be the same? Will you be able to trust your body to take the intense pressure you'll put it through? These questions will go through your mind, and you'll never have your answers until you're back on the court. If you're ever injured, once your doctor clears you, you *have* to get back out there, get back to work, cast away your doubts and fears, and set your mind at ease. The key is definitely exercising patience and trusting the rehabilitation process. If you return to the court too soon, you'll run the risk of injuring yourself all over again. It'll be tough, but you can *typically* return to your former glory after an injury.

I know a lot about the physical and psychological effects of sports injuries because I was unlucky enough to have one in 2010. I had microfractures in both knees, requiring me to have surgery. I was so impatient to be done with rehab and get back on the court that I came back too early; my game and my body definitely suffered because of this. Consequently, I ended up getting cut from my D-League team, the Sioux Falls Skyforce, in January 2012. About a month before getting cut, I noticed my agent had stopped answering my calls and definitely stopped calling me as frequently. Once I got cut from my team, our lines of communication only got worse. He soon stopped answering my calls and messages altogether. Here it is, 2017, and I still haven't heard from my former agent since before I was cut from that team!

Though that experience hurt, it also taught me a great deal. Sometimes things happen in life and you just have to roll with it and do all you can to bounce back. I was abandoned by my agent at one of the lowest points in my career, but I was in a much better position than the *first* time I was without an agent and looking for a team. I now had options and could be a little more discerning.

I was also way more knowledgeable about dealing with agents and knowing what I want out of people who represent me.

I want an agent who makes it plain that he or she works for me. I don't want to feel like I have to hunt people down if they work for me. It's also important for my agent to be completely transparent about my situation and my options. I don't want anyone selling me a dream, nor do I want anyone making moves on my behalf without at least discussing them with me first. Some players aren't like me.

Some are cool without knowing details and want to just sign on the dotted line. I have a more hands-on approach, especially concerning what goes on with my bank account, paying my own bills, and having an understanding about if a team is interested in me or not. Your career is important. You should be involved all aspects of your career and your life. You don't have to have the same hands-on approach as I do, but you shouldn't be ignorant of anything your agent is doing for you. Get involved in your career! Never be afraid to ask questions, especially when it comes to your livelihood, especially with people who are supposed to work for you. You often hear about people saying their agent, manager, accountant, etc. stole from them.

Things like that happen because these people weren't required to be transparent, or because they were trusted so fully that they took advantage of their employer. At the end of day, you have to be aware of what's going on, because it's *your* money and *your* life that will be affected. Pay attention to and be aware of every decision someone makes for you, whether it be financial or otherwise.

"Using Social Media"

So what happened after two microfracture surgeries, having my agent dump me, and being cut by my team? Moving to Libya, of course! Libya is a large, oil-rich, desert country in Africa, with a population of a little over six million people. Libya gained notoriety mostly due to its former dictator, Muammar Gaddafi. Not many people know about Libya's basketball culture. I personally had no knowledge of Libyan basketball leagues until I went there.

So how in the hell did I end up playing basketball in Libya? I leveraged the power of social media, despite not really being an active social media user. I didn't have an agent or a team, and I felt like my search for an agent wasn't going as I'd hoped, so I decided to stop looking for one. I thought maybe I'd retire from basketball and get into coaching, but before I completely gave up on my hoop dreams, I figured it couldn't hurt to try it on my own for a while. So, I took my most recent highlight film and posted it on a free agent networking page on Facebook. My video got a couple of likes and a few reposts here and there. Maybe a month or two after posting my highlight film, an Egyptian coach named Tarek Wasfy liked the video and sent me a private message about joining his team, Al Hilal of the Libyan Basketball League. Just when I thought my career was about to be over, I was given another shot at fulfilling my dreams!

You never know what opportunities will come your way, but you better always try your best to be ready for them! I went from having no agent, no team, and thinking I was going to be forced to retire to being handpicked by an international team. Sometimes you just have to step out on faith and try one more time, even when it seems like all is lost.

Being picked up by the team in Libya in the way I was is also a testament to the wonders of social media. If you are trying to market yourself without an agent, first and foremost, remember to believe in yourself. It may sound corny, but know that no one is going to have faith in you if you don't have faith in yourself. Secondly, don't let anyone deter you from going after what you truly want. Thirdly, and perhaps most importantly, use your resources! Take your old highlight films, statistics, whatever you have access to, and put together a player profile package. Keep spare copies on hand, and post your videos to all social media platforms. Then, get your friends and family to repost your videos. All it takes is one coach, one general manager, one person in power to become interested in you. Don't be defeated or discouraged if you find yourself doing it alone. It's great if you have a good agent in your corner, but you *can* do it on your own.

How To Make It To The NBA

SECTION 4:

How to Make It to the NBA

You look up at the timer as you dribble the ball down the court. There are twenty seconds left in the game, and your team is down by one point. You notice the beads of sweat cascading off the forehead of the opposing guard as you both glare at each other, eye to eye. He quickly swipes at the sweat with the back of his hand and continues to gaze at you like a predator would his prey, refusing to let you out of his sight. The crowd watches on with bated breath. You've waited your whole life to be in an NBA finals game, and here you are, in

Game 7, with the outcome literally in your hands. A faction of the opposing crowd boo and chant against you, praying to see your team fail. It's make or break time, and you'll either become the hero or the villain. Another glance at the clock shows that you've managed to waste another ten seconds. You have to move quickly! Your shooting guard tries to come off a screen that's set by your power forward and is struggling to shake off his defender. He's not an option. You notice your center posting up against the opposition's center, ready to receive the ball, but then you remember how you'd fed him the ball in Game 3 and he missed that easy layup, costing your team the game. Your coach blasted you for that pass in the locker room. Your only other option is your small forward. When you look at him, however, his eyes look tired and he almost looks like he hopes you don't pass him the ball, so you waive that option away. After seeing that the clock now has less than seven seconds on it, you know it has to be you who finishes this game. You stare your opposition down, left to right crossover and one more escape dribble, then shoot a jumper from the baseline. It seems as though everyone in the arena holds their breath as you all watch the ball travel through the air. The ball hits the left rim, rolls around, then...falls through the net! The buzzer sounds and the crowd erupts in joy, the atmosphere electric and dazzling...and then you awaken from your nap.

I've had that recurring dream many times since falling in love with basketball. I'm sure every aspiring player out there can relate. You dream of being in the NBA, being in the finals, and making the game-winning shot. Or stopping a potentially game-winning shot with a monster block. Or getting the rebound that helped your team fast break and win the game. Or giving the smooth assist for the game winning shot. You get my point! The scenario can be played in many different ways, but the message is simple: you want to be the star of an NBA franchise, delivering when your team needs you the most.

Getting into the NBA is arguably the pinnacle of a basketball player's career. The NBA is where the fame, acclaim, and money is. The NBA also houses some of the world's most enthusiastic fans. Being in the NBA means you're one of the best of the best. As a kid, I'd dream of seeing my face on billboards, having people wear jerseys with my last name emblazoned on the back, and having fans chant heartily as I jogged down the court. Virtually every kid with hoop dreams wants to play in the NBA, and I was no exception.

Before I talk about my time in the NBA, let me tell you how I made it to the NBA. Again, the D-League is the NBA's official minor league basketball organization. Many current or former NBA players have either started their careers in the D-League or spent some time there at some point. My professional career started out in the D-League in 2006. I didn't have the acclaim, fame, or even the money, but I was still a professional basketball player! I never truly made a name for myself in college, and most people only knew me when I mentioned that I'd played alongside Ronnie Brewer, the 14th draft pick of the 2006 NBA Draft. When people did recognize me, however, they knew me for my great defensive skills.

I was drafted into the D-League in 2006 by

the Dakota Wizards, where I spent two years. My first year was very successful, with my team winning the 2007 D-League Championship. I returned to the D-League in 2008, but I left in the middle of the season to play overseas with the Barons LMT in Riga, Latvia. I won another championship with my Latvian team. I returned back to the D-league for a third year, at which time I was traded to the Utah Flash. In my third year with the Flash, I was able to showcase my skills a lot more while exclusively playing point guard instead of splitting time between playing point and shooting guard; this caused more teams to take interest in me. My time with the Flash was so successful that it led to me being selected for the D- League All Star team and eventually a call-up to the NBA with the Charlotte Bobcats! A call-up is simply a 10-day trial with an NBA team during which they evaluate you and decide if they want to add you to their roster. You typically do 20 consecutive days, then the team decides if they want to keep you or send you back to the D-League. I signed a two-year, non-guaranteed deal which stated that my money was fully guaranteed after my call- up, and that the next season my contract would be based upon me making the roster again and making it through a certain date with the team to be guaranteed again. I was released in training camp after my first season with the Bobcats, so I returned back to the D- League for the next season. Unfortunately, I injured myself while taking a jumpshot during a preseason game with the Utah Flash. This was how I ended up having to have microstructure surgery on my knees. My surgeries not only sidelined me for a year, they also took away a lot of my self-assurance. Consequently, my next two post-surgery years in the D-League were very unsuccessful. Eventually, thankfully, I was cut from the Skyforce which allowed me to sit out the rest of the year. I had been a dominant D-League player the years before my call-up, and had even lived my dream of being in the NBA. When I had to have surgery, I had to come down from my high and reevaluate things in order to truly get better. I had to figure out what was really right for me in the end. My career has had its ups and downs, and has definitely taught me patience!

Before I had surgery, I wanted things done right away and I never wanted to wait for things to work out. But I've since learned to respect life's processes. My recovery *forced* me to sit down and be patient and understand that while things may not always turn out how I want them to, they'll always work out in the end. After having my surgery, things changed. Though I eventually regained my confidence, the D-League just wasn't the same for me anymore. Some coaches still believed in me, but I could tell some didn't. My game was definitely affected, and without even realizing it, I began to shut down in some ways. I knew I had to make a change within my career.

Some people viewed the NBA D- League as being subpar to the NBA. While the two leagues are very different, they also have many similarities. Like the NBA, the D-League was very demanding. Most teams accommodate players with a two- bedroom, two-bathroom apartment, which they share with one other teammate. You don't have to pay for room and board, but you do have to pay for food and personal items. Sometimes you get to enjoy the perks of free or discounted food from various restaurants that have partnered with the team.

Travel demands might be the worst part of being a D-League player, and I'd argue the same for being in the NBA. You might have a game Friday night at 7:00pm and another game, in another city, Saturday at 7:00pm. But for the Saturday 7:00pm game, your flight departs at 4:00am! So we'd often play a game, go home to pack, try to get as much sleep as possible, then head to the airport around 2:30am. Like I said, it was very demanding.

As far as D-League salaries are concerned, there were three basic pay scales at the time: A) $32,000 for six months, B) $24,000 for six months, or C) $12,000 for six months. D-League players only get paid for six months out of the year. The other six months are typically spent preparing for the following season, so most players only have that one source of income (though I highly recommend investing). Though I hope the pay has gotten better, most players stay in the D- League because of its close proximity to the NBA, not the paycheck. There's no way your average person would bust his ass everyday for $12,000 a year without the possibility of a huge payoff! The allure of possibly being a call-up to the NBA is what keeps most players committed. The fame, big checks, and accolades are so close within your grasp you can taste it! Every D-League player hopes to get a call- up to the NBA, so the (hopefully brief) paycheck sacrifice seems worth it. A lot of guys also go to the D-League to develop their skills (again, the "D" stands for "developmental") and make themselves more marketable for NBA teams. You can get into NBA training camps or play with an NBA team for summer leagues, so the D-League definitely has some advantages. The biggest disadvantage, of course, was the pay scale. Players made about $4,000 per month in the D-League when you can easily make more than twice that playing overseas. But again, the NBA is the league everyone wants to be in. D-League players simply deal with the salary in hopes of making it big someday.

"Life in the D-League"

My life as a D-League player was pretty normal. The D-League is run like the NBA, with its amazing fans and demanding schedule, but you aren't in the spotlight as much as an NBA player, so life pretty much stays the same. I made sure I went to practice on time, ate healthily, and got my necessary rest. I'd go to the movies, out to dinner or bowling with my teammates, then come home and chill. As I said, I'm not much of a party guy for the most part, so life for me was still pretty low-key. Although being a player could be very taxing, it was easy to do my job. I made sure I stayed out of trouble and used my common sense. I'd recommend that anyone interested in being a D-League player find a nice hobby doing whatever makes you happy because when you get off the road, life can be a little boring, especially if you don't have family and friends to keep you occupied.

The biggest thing you can do to maximize your opportunities with the D- League is to be ready whenever you're put in the game. The window to get that call- up to play in the NBA is very small because there are so many guys trying to make that awesome transition. When the opportunity presents itself, take full advantage of it. One thing that is important to understand is that NBA teams aren't necessarily interested in you because you're a star player scoring 30 points every game. A lot of times D- League (now G League) players are brought in because a star NBA player is hurt and they need you to be the backup for the backup. Most of the time, NBA teams simply need you to play a role. With that being said, you still better play the best basketball you've ever played! No need to try to play superstar, but when you're called up, do what is asked of you, pick your spots, and be as polished and aggressive as you can be. You may initially have gotten a call-up to fill a void, but your tenacity, professionalism, and skills may very well secure you a permanent spot on an NBA roster.

"Overseas or D-League?"

I was in the middle of my 2007- 2008 D-League season when my agent notified me of the offer from Barons LMT in Latvia. I knew absolutely nothing about Latvia or Latvian basketball, so I asked my teammates if any of them were familiar. A few trusted friends gave some very useful information, and that information coupled with the salary the Barons LMT offered convinced me to give it a try. The potential for an NBA call-up was on my mind at the time, of course, but it didn't seem imminent. So, I packed my bags and went to play in Latvia.

I loved everything about living in Latvia! The food was amazing, the people were kind, and my teammates and organization were welcoming. I was able to experience a new culture and see a little of the world. It was initially a bit difficult adjusting to living in a country where I didn't speak the language of the majority of its occupants, but it got easier. I was around my teammates most of the time, and most of them spoke English and were able to translate. At first, the most daunting thing about living in Latvia had nothing to do with the people, food, or culture. The thing that took the most getting used to was my bank account! It was overwhelming to see that much money in my account at one time, and I had to quickly learn how to manage my funds over there so I wouldn't come home broke! You might have the urge to ball out, but remember, those checks only come half of the year. Don't mismanage your money and end up assed out for the rest of the year!

One thing I did to save money while I was in Latvia was try not to eat out. You really do save a lot of money when you meal plan and eat at home. And of course I still didn't go out partying much. You typically only get paid once a month while working overseas, usually at the beginning or the end of the month. The hard part about only being paid once a month is that sometimes you come in contact with some organizations who don't pay on time, so it's especially important to manage your money well. Not all international teams are like this, though. You just have to research potential teams and their pay history. I do believe that players consider their financial situation over everything when deciding to pay overseas or not. Basketball is a job, and we play to provide for ourselves and our families. So while the allure of being so close to the NBA is strong, and most people don't want to leave their family and friends for a foreign country, a lot of players make the prudent decision to play overseas to make more money. Before going overseas, though, consider how close you really might be to getting into the NBA. How is the dialogue between your agent and general managers and coaches of NBA teams? How well did you play in the summer league? How close are you to really getting that call-up? If you feel that you're close to getting a call-up, you might want to take a chance, not go overseas, and hope for the best. Everyone's situation is different, but finances and chances of you landing in the NBA should be the main deciding factors in whether you choose to go overseas or tough it out in the D- League. You definitely want to be ready for whatever opportunity comes your way.

You also have to be prepared for the consequences of your decision. If you stay in the D-League in lieu of going overseas, you'll miss out on a lot of extra money. If you go overseas and leave the D-League, you might miss out on a once-in-a- lifetime call-up. Think quickly about what's best for you, feel secure in your decision, and try not to have any regrets!

Getting a call-up to the NBA from the D-League is a joyous, surreal experience. You feel like all the effort and time you've put in over the years is finally being recognized. I still remember my call-up like it was yesterday. It was during my third year in the D-League when I received that early morning call from my agent. I was annoyed at being awakened at 6:00am, Mountain Time, especially considering I had a game later that night and had to be up in a few hours for my morning shootaround. I answered and immediately started chewing him out for calling so early. He let me get it all out, then gave me news that got me excited all over again, but in a good way. My agent told me not to play in that night's game because I'd been called-up to the Charlotte Bobcats! I felt overwhelmed with emotion and immediately started crying with my agent still on the phone. Still dizzy with happiness from the news, I hung up with my agent and called my mom right away. It was definitely one of the best days of my life, and she was nothing but supportive and delighted for me. I sat there and cried on the phone all over again with my mom, my emotions spilling over.

The rest of that day seemed to go by in a very slow blur. Many of my teammates and people connected to the Utah Flash at the time congratulated me and wished me the best when I went to shootaround that morning.

I didn't know what to think on that flight to Charlotte. I felt that all the hard work I'd put in over the years after leaving Arkansas finally counted for something. All the long practices, all the time spent in the gym, maintaining three points and five assists per game, it all counted for something. My determination and faith, and the faith of my loved ones, all came to fruition with this, my biggest achievement. I'd finally made it!

Being in Charlotte was a blessing and I learned a lot from the experience. I didn't get in any games or dress out my first few weeks, but I actually played in the last six games of the season! The more time I was given in a game, the better I played. I finished my last game of the season with a career high of 12 points, 5 rebounds, 4 assists, and 2 steals! That game and those stats gave me a lot of confidence, especially considering I didn't get much practice time in because we were trying to make the playoffs. I was fortunate to be surrounded by an amazing team that wanted me to succeed in signing with the team. I proved myself after two, ten-day contracts and signed to join the Bobcats roster. Signing day was *the* most important day of my life. I'll never forget that day, my wonderful teammates, or the elated feeling that was radiating from my body.

The biggest lesson I learned from being in the NBA, and something all sports fans should learn, is that every player on a professional team is there for a reason. A lot of times people think if a player doesn't get in games it automatically means he's sorry and shouldn't be on the team. Trust me, if a guy is on the roster, he *deserves* to be on the roster. Every player that fills spots 1-15 on a roster serves a role. There's a reason why teams have 15 players, even though there are only 5 positions. There may be two players in your position who the team views as being better than you, but that doesn't mean you're not a great player. The NBA is too competitive, and there are too many G League guys waiting for their chance to shine for teams to fill their rosters with sorry players.

You never really notice how hard you're working until you see some of your favorite players working just as hard. They push you, and you push them, and everyone wants to be the best. I met some great guys during my time in Charlotte, and I'll always cherish it. There's nothing like the camaraderie of an NBA team with everyone encouraging and challenging you to do your best so your team can reach its ultimate goal: winning an NBA championship.

"So What's the Difference?"

There isn't much of a difference between playing overseas, in the G League, or in the NBA. I do think that playing overseas is the most different, because overseas organizations are more team-oriented. International teams import players to enhance their chances of winning, so the workload for the imports (oftentimes American players) is very demanding.

Games are a lot shorter overseas. You play four, 10-minute quarters as opposed to the four, 12- minute quarters of the NBA and G League. You practice twice a day when you play overseas, and the resources to recover and take care your body aren't as widely and readily available.

Playing professionally is a lot faster- paced than playing in college. Playing in the NBA differs from the G League in that the guys are a lot more experienced and have honed their craft. G League and NBA games are very similarly paced. But, it's all about how you prepare yourself. You'll be ready for any league, and any pace, as long as you do all you can to be ready to perform at any level.

"Just a Regular Guy"

Contrary to what people may think, most NBA players lead pretty normal lifestyles; I did, at least. A typical day would consist of me going to practice in the morning for about an hour and a half. After practice I'd shoot extra shots or practice whatever drills I felt I needed to work on. Then, I'd sit in a cold tub followed by a shower, and I was pretty much free for the rest of the day unless I had a community appearance. If the team didn't provide lunch for us, I'd go get something to eat, then go home and chill. My days were very low-key and nothing spectacular. I guess one of the most lavish things I enjoyed as an NBA player was the team travel. We flew on spacious, chartered planes with deliciously catered food. Once we touched down, we'd be whisked off to a beautiful, luxurious hotel. I really loved NBA travel, especially compared to D-League travel where we took commercial flights and weren't given as many amenities.

"What Do NBA Teams Expect?"

The most NBA teams expect of you is that you continue to do what got you there in the first place, and that you always strive for improvement. The NBA doesn't want you to change who you are as a player, but they do want you to be able to perform at a higher level within the team system. Whatever you've always been good at, refine those skills and shine. If you're known for your defensive skills, be the best defensive player. If you're a great rebounder, strive to *always* be the one getting those rebounds. If you're a pretty good three-point shooter, work to become your team's *best* three-point shooter! Simply do the things that got you there in the first place. If you're coming from the G League, it may take a while for a team to stick with you. Sometimes you'll secure a 10-day contract and then they'll send you back. They might bring you back again, or another team will notice you and bring you aboard. All you can do for your part is stay consistent and always be ready to perform at your best. All it takes is one team to sign you for the rest of the year to catapult your career to the next level. You can end up securing a NBA spot, or perform well enough to put you in a position to make more money overseas.

"Guaranteed vs. Non-Guaranteed Contracts"

There are guaranteed and non- guaranteed contracts in the NBA, as negotiated by your agent. Guaranteed contracts are ideal, but your agent can negotiate your contract to where a large portion of your money will become guaranteed if you happen to be cut, injured, or traded. If you're still on the team roster after a certain date in the NBA, your contract can become fully guaranteed. A lot of free agents tend to have non-guaranteed contracts. They have to work a lot harder and minimize mistakes in an effort to obtain a guaranteed contract.

Most of the players who have guaranteed years are first round draft picks or veteran players whose agents secured a guaranteed deal. Contracts can be very tedious, but definitely beneficial. Make sure you perform at your best and that your agent does all he or she can to try to secure a guaranteed contract for you, as they give you more financial stability. If you were originally non-guaranteed, your performance and your agent's hard work can secure a guaranteed contract. If you aren't performing as well as people think you should but you have a guaranteed contract, your money is secure. It's definitely up to the team to decide how they want to proceed with non- guaranteed deals, but you and your agent have to do all you can to have things work out in your favor.

"Never Lose the Foundation"

I truly believe in the cliché phrase "never forget where you came from." If you become successful, try not to detour too far from the things, people, and behaviors that made you successful. So, every summer up until my surgery, I returned to the University of Arkansas to work out with my former roommate, Ronnie Brewer (9-year NBA veteran), Vincent Hunter (10-year veteran overseas), and strength coach, Kelly Lambert. Ronnie's dad, Ron Brewer, who was a member of the University of Arkansas's "Triplets" and an 8-year NBA veteran, trained us on our skill work. We'd workout doing the same weight program a few days a week every summer, and I'd often come at night to get extra shots up. I worked on consistently shooting my three-pointer, different ball-handling drills, and even playing against guys in the NBA to try to extend my range and improve my game.

I was having a great summer in 2010 then Kelly Lambert moved on to be the Memphis

Grizzlies' strength and conditioning coach in the fall of 2010, so I was no longer under his guidance. I lost a bit of confidence in myself due to not having him to train me anymore feeling without him my strength would not be the same. It also showed during my play. Two and a half years after my surgery, I met Kelly in Atlanta. He put me through a vigorous workout and explained the program in detail and made me believe that I didn't need him to do the program. That workout with Kelly gave me the confidence I needed to get back on track with my workouts. After closely following his program, I definitely noticed a difference in my game. I was way more explosive on the court than I'd been in previous years. If it wasn't for me keeping in touch with the people I'd know in my past, my post-surgery game may have never truly improved.

When everything seemed to be going wrong, I tried to stay positive. I also made sure to keep myself around people who wished me well and wanted to see me become a better basketball player. Staying positive and surrounding myself with good people is what I needed to push me to better my situation after the injury. It's what every person needs after an injury. Injuries are a part of the game. There are only a select few who are blessed to have never been injured within their careers.

Again, one of the most important things for you to do after an injury is to be patient! Everyone's body recovers differently. Take rehab seriously and do whatever the training staff asks of you. The only way you'll get better physically is to stay strong mentally. Progress doesn't happen overnight, and you won't return back to 100percent right away, but having the mental fortitude to keep pushing through the pain is what will help you recover. Remember: stay positive, be patient, and keep good people around you. Stick with the people who have been there all along and you'll be able to face anything.

"When Love Calls"

Like most young men, I dated and played the

field. Even though I don't party a lot, I definitely enjoyed my fair share of the club scene. All that completely changed when I fell in love. I started to look at life differently, and I considered her in every decision I made. I cared about how certain jobs would affect our relationship, and I'd often ask her advice on career moves. I'd finally found something besides basketball that really mattered to me.

Fast forward a year and a half into our relationship, we broke up. It was one of the toughest times in my personal life. It affected me more than any of my career setbacks, more than any woman ever had. Immediately after we broke up, I contemplated suicide on the 16-hour drive from her house back to Atlanta. I fell into a depression, and of course this affected my career. I'd recently been cut from my team after trying to reestablish myself after my surgery, my agent had abandoned me, and I lost who I thought was the love of my life. I was at the lowest point of my life. Everything felt upside down.

Thankfully, I still had my amazing support system. Never, ever, lose touch with the people who have always been there for you, because they will be the ones to help build you back up when everything feels like it has fallen apart. Be open to love again because in those dark moments you never know what may be waiting for you behind those shadows. I overcame heartbreak, regrouped, and refocused my energy on getting myself in shape, both mentally and physically. Sometimes you have to go through the pain to find peace, and I'm grateful that I did.

"Party Hard, Party Smart"

When teams are thinking of adding you to their rosters, they'll actually go back to high school and college to learn about you and your character. How did you get along with former coaches, teammates, or professors? Did you get into trouble a lot? What do people have to say about your character? Teams take all of these things into consideration.

My advice, especially for you up- and-coming athletes, is to be smart. Have fun, party, and enjoy yourself, but don't do anything that can jeopardize your dreams. Don't put yourself in positions or hang around people that aren't good for your image. Don't get yourself labeled a party animal, bad guy, or hot head. Don't be the player who's always in and out of the media or clubs. No team wants to be affiliated with a PR nightmare. Have fun and enjoy the fruits of your labor, because you'll definitely work hard. Just be smart and try to project positivity, remember your values and what you stand for. You not only represent yourself, you represent your family, your community, and your team. It can be a lot to shoulder, but as an athlete, you have to be prepared for it. So party, but party wisely!

"What's Next?"

One thing everyone needs to understand is that an athlete's career span is very short. The average career for an NBA player is three years, and then you're out. I only spent a year there myself and I haven't been back. It can be a cold, cut- throat game if you don't know how to handle it. My advice is to keep your God first, eat and train well, and stay ready. Your body is a machine; if you take care of it, it will take care of you. All the little things you may think are unimportant right now, like icing your knees after a game, for example, will become very important once you turn thirty and have had years of running up and down the court. Everything you do (or don't do) to take care of yourself will play a role in your future. Take care of yourself now to extend your career to as long as *you* want it to be.

One day, basketball is going to end for you. Be ready for that day. You have the resources out there to take care of your body, mind, and money, so use them! Think about life after basketball, because if you play your cards right, you'll have countless options. You can coach, teach, train, own a sports facility, go into politics to help your community, anything! Find sound investments while you're still getting steady paychecks to ensure a flow of income after basketball. Get to know your passions outside of basketball and formulate a plan for what you'll do when your professional basketball career ends. Thinking about the future now will help to avoid financial issues and depression when the hoop dreams are over. Make as many friends as you can and develop a sound network with coaches, teammates, and trainers. You never know who might be able to help you actualize your post- basketball dreams!

How To Make It To The NBA

CLOSING

I've had an amazing time traveling down memory lane, especially when I think about all I've overcome to get to where I am today. I didn't have recruiters beating down my door, nor was I a #1 draft pick, but I made it to a D1 university and to every basketball player's ultimate dream, the NBA. These days, I'm rounding out the last year of my professional basketball career. When I retire, I'll focus heavily on enjoying the development and management of my portfolio as a real estate investor and hopefully meeting you in person one day to share my story hands on. I've had my highs and lows, but I have truly been honored to experience every minute of my journey. I hope I've provided some insight and that my story will help you avoid some of the pitfalls I encountered. It's a beautiful life, so work hard, play hard, and get out there and make it happen!